AF262908

COLORSSS

Deborah A. Hutchinson, PhD

Peanut Butter Publishing
206-860-4900
info@peanutbutterpublishing.com
www.peanutbutterpublishing.com

For Emilia and Madeline,
both of whom
bring so much color
to my life.

One little egg, as white as can be, could give rise to snakes of many colors, you see.

Would you be surprised
if someone had said
that some snakes
are quite red?

Others are fit for Halloween, with nothing but orange and **black** to be seen.

While some seem
to say, "Hello!"
with their scales so
bright yellow.

Some snakes are shades of **blue**, complete with a rainbow hue.

And if you don't blink,
you might find some
snakes that are not
only green but pink!

So appreciate the
beauty of nature all
around you,

not only in furry
creatures...

...but in scaly ones too!

Still curiousss?

Read on!

Why be colorful at all?

Snakes can be found in every color of the rainbow. Why do you think that is?

Some snakes have colors and patterns that blend into their surroundings. This helps them hide from predators to avoid becoming another animal's lunch.

Others use their bright colors to warn predators that they may be dangerous and should be left alone.

If the snake's colors fail to protect it from a predator's attack, the snake may actively defend itself by striking or fleeing. Instead of fight or flight, it may bite or slither!

Venomous or nonvenomous?

There are more than 3,000 species of snakes in the world, and most are nonvenomous, meaning that they lack venom. If a nonvenomous snake bites you, it may hurt, but the risk of injury is small.

Venomous snakes can inject venom with their teeth. Although venomous snakes can be dangerous, most snakes are not aggressive. If you're unsure whether a snake is nonvenomous or venomous, give it space so that it does not feel the need to bite to defend itself. Venomous snakes would rather save their venom for its primary purpose—hunting for a tasty snack!

Snakes should be admired from a distance, for all their colors and beauty, especially if they are venomous—like the one to the right.

Venomous or poisonous?

Although many people refer to *venomous* snakes as being *poisonous,* these words do not mean the same thing. Venomous snakes can inject toxins with their teeth, whereas poisonous snakes contain chemicals in their bodies that taste terrible and could make a predator sick if it tried to make a meal of the snake. In fact, some snakes are both venomous *and* poisonous—like the one to the right!

Venoms and poisons can be dangerous, but in small doses, they can be used to treat human diseases. Scientists have found many uses for the venoms and poisons found in nature, and many more remain to be discovered. To make future discoveries possible, we must preserve natural habitats so that all creatures can thrive. The next time you see a snake, be sure to say, "Thank you!"

A note to parents and caregivers

Thank you for purchasing this book and for teaching today's children about the importance of appreciating all the colors of nature.

I have witnessed children react positively toward snakes until they see an adult near them recoil. When that happens, the child's demeanor tends to pivot from curiosity to fear. Instead of teaching children to fear snakes, I would much prefer to see adults model how to respect nature in all of its forms.

Snakes play a crucial role in the ecosystems where they live, and they provide us with many benefits that often go unrecognized. Snakes reduce the numbers of pests that can carry diseases (rodents) or damage gardens (slugs). The toxins from venomous snakes have been used to treat a wide variety of conditions in humans, including high blood pressure, cancer, and diabetes.

Many additional benefits of nature remain to be discovered, and the necessary first step in realizing those benefits is to protect and preserve organisms and the environments in which they live.

You've already taken an important step by teaching children why nature is so valuable. You can do more by donating your time or other resources to help conservation groups that work locally, nationally, and internationally.

"In the end, we will conserve only what we love,
we will love only what we understand,
and we will understand only what we are taught."
—Baba Dioum

List of snake species photographed in this book, in order of appearance:

A. *Heterodon platirhinos* (Eastern hognose snake from USA)

B. *Rhabdophis tigrinus* (Japanese keelback)

C. *Euprepiophis conspicillata* (Japanese rat snake)

D. *Heterodon platirhinos* (Eastern hognose snake from USA)

E. *Pantherophis alleghaniensis* (Eastern rat snake from USA)

F. *Rhabdophis tigrinus* (Japanese keelback)

G. *Rhabdophis nigrocinctus* (Black-banded keelback from Thailand)

H. *Rhabdophis tigrinus* (Japanese keelback)

I. *Rhabdophis tigrinus* (Japanese keelback)

J. *Gloydius blomhoffii* (Mamushi from Japan)

K. *Ovophis okinavensis* (Okinawan pit viper from Japan)

L. *Rhabdophis tigrinus* (Japanese keelback)

Ssssee you later!